Take Comfort

Take comfort in your darkest hour from all
that comes your way—from every little
gleam of light that brightens up the day.

The scent of flowers, the joy of music and
the song of birds. The magic world of
books: the precious treasury of words.

Life offers compensations. They are round
you everywhere. The gifts of friendship
and of love, of hope and faith and prayer.

Consolations of the spirit, blessings great
and small. The things through which God
speaks to you. Take comfort from them all.

See in

Bare Boughs

The bare boughs reach across the window
pane. It's hard to think they'll ever live
again. It seems to me a thing incredible—
that there could be so great a miracle.

So dead they look seen from this firelit room.
Dark and stark against the wintry gloom.
And yet this day unto that gnarled old tree—
there came a blackbird with a prophecy.

Out of the greyness of the sky he flew—into
the branches where the cold winds blew . . .
And boldly he prophesied this wondrous
thing—filling the garden with a dream of
spring.

The Same Old Road

We think we have a claim on life. We
think we have a right—to comfort, pleasure
and security . . . But every time Utopia
begins to loom in sight—we find some snag
in our philosophy.

Which goes to prove that there's no easy
creed, no quick new way—our plans and
and our ambitions to achieve. The
fundamental laws of life are still the same
today. We have to give if we are to receive.

And so in spite of all the so-called progress
we have made—We find we have to bear
our human load . . . The simple truths of
life we cannot cancel or evade. Salvation
lies along the same old road.

The Music is to Come

The woods are silent and austere, no song
breaks through the trees. No golden note
comes rippling on the bleak and wintry
breeze—But the music is to come! We
know it to be true. There'll be thrushes in
the copse and skylarks in the blue.

We too have our silences, our songless
sunless years. We too have our winter tides
of trouble and of tears. But we always know
in spite of sorrow and of pain—that the
music is to come.

. . . The heart will sing again.

You Can't Have Everything

You'll never find perfection for the world's
not made like that. And if it were I think
in time you'd find life rather flat. So don't
expect a heaven. Leave your grumbles on
the mat. You can't have everything.

Do not feel disgruntled, disappointed and
depressed—if a plan you followed has not
turned out for the best. Do not brood on
losses, but recall how you've been blessed. . .
You can't have everything.

In those we live and work with there are
faults that irritate—but don't forget that
though there may be much to aggravate—
There is oh so much to love and to
appreciate. You can't have everything.

It Always Comes Out Fine Again

Despair is sin. So never let it steal into
your mind. Though you've taken many
blows and Fate has been unkind—Things
will take a turn if you can hold out long
enough.

The outlook may be grim and gloomy and
the going rough—but when you reach the
valley where the shadows round you close—
it always comes out fine again, for that's the
way life goes.

Don't despair because you cannot see a patch of blue. There is better country out beyond the present view.

Happiness awaits the heart that keeps its Faith alight—though there seems to be no promise and no gleam of light—The very moment when you think that God's forgotten you—is the moment just before the sun comes breaking through.

Wonderful

Shadows of prophetic darkness lie across
the world. But underneath the hawthorn
hedge a primrose has uncurled. And what
could be more wonderful and more
mysterious—than this tiny miracle that God
has wrought for us?

In this age when Hell's own noises beat
about our ears—and new inventions fill
our hearts with horror and with fears. It's
good to be reminded that in spite of
everything—Nature's quiet work goes on
and nightingales still sing.

These things are more marvellous than
engines, bombs and jets: Apple blossom,
daffodils and April violets. In a world of
ugly things, of speed and strife and strain.
It is sweet to contemplate a primrose in a
lane.

If

If nature's laws broke down this year. We'd have no golden harvest here. If buds and pods were not unsealed in the orchard and the field—there'd be no crops for winter's store and famine would be at the door—if the earth should fail us now and bring no life to stalk or bough.

If God forgot to send the spring—and the birds all ceased to sing. If summer's flowers did not unclose . . . Imagine June without a rose! The gardens would be dead and bare—with no beauty anywhere. We take for granted all these things: the seed that grows, the bird that sings. Praise Him from Whom all blessings start—with a glad and grateful heart.

The Twilight of the Year

Autumn's touch is soft and gentle. Slowly
do the seasons turn. Green leaves change to
red and gold on bush and tree and wayside
fern. It is hard to think of snow and of the
woodlands stark and sere—-as October fades
away into the twilight of the year.

Peace and plenty and contentment crown
this rich and lovely hour—when we gather
in the last of Summer's good and golden
dower . . . One by one the roses drop in
gardens drenched with diamond dew—and
along the village street there drifts the
woodsmoke grey and blue.

Slow are nature's transformations in this
cool and temperate Isle. Winter stands upon
the threshold, yet we bask in Autumn's
smile . . . If we could only live like this we'd
never fear the changing scene—but face the
twilight of our lives with hearts untroubled
and serene.

Thankful Every Morning

Be thankful every morning when you wake
to life anew. No matter how you feel or
what may lie ahead of you. Don't expect the
worst to happen. Be an optimist. Be
grateful and be happy. Give your thoughts
an upward twist.

When you wake don't start to count your
troubles with a sigh. Count your blessings up
instead and they will multiply. You will be
surprised how many lovely things you'll
find—once you start to search into the
corners of your mind.

Make a pleasure of your work, enjoy your
leisure too. Take each day as if it is a gift
bestowed on you . . . You can choose if you
will live it being bright or sad. It's the mental
attitude makes life seem good or bad.

In Between the Crosses

Sorrows come. But life is not all trials and tribulations. In between the sorrows there are many consolations . . . Deserts of affliction can be dark and dreadful places . . . But here and there between the rocks you'll find a green oasis.

In between the times of trouble and of desolation—There are good and happy years that come as compensation . . . When you look back on the past remembering your losses—Don't forget the flowers God planted in between the crosses.

Take Note

Take note of all the lovely things that
happen in the day—the unexpected
treasures you discover by the way . . . The
things that make you happy and the things
that make you smile—the things that make
you feel that what you do is well worth
while.

Take note and jot them down upon the
page of memory. And when the day has
ended add them up and you will see—They
outnumber all the things that made you
frown and fret—the irritating things that
made you worried and upset.

Every little thing that makes for comfort
and content: the helping hand, the word of
kindness and encouragement. The small
adventures of the day that go to make the
fun. The providential happenings . . . Take
note of every one.

Survival

Looking at the frozen earth so hard and cold
and bare—you wonder how the seeds will
ever come to life down there . . . You can't
imagine how out of that grave of leaden
clay—there will come the glory of a
resurrection day.

You can't believe that you will ever see a
new green tip. You'd think that everything
would die in winter's cruel grip . . . The
garden wears a mask of death and yet it is
alive. The bulbs are buried in the dark—but
somehow they survive.

And when to someone dearly loved you say
a last goodbye—you feel at first it is the
end—but love can never die . . . Hopes lie
buried and it seems the clouds will never
part—but time that brings the flowers to
life will heal a broken heart.

Advent

As the winter deepens and the shortest day
draws near—Advent comes to give a glory
to the dying year—and strikes a chord of
hope that turns our hearts expectantly—
towards the time that marks the greatest day
in history.

Drear December opens with the threat of
frost and snow—but the scene is lightened
by a strange and lovely glow—for Advent is
the herald that foretells the wondrous thing
—and bids the world look forward to the
coming of the King.

The Gates of Memory

When I lift the latch upon the Gates of
Memory—I find I am surrounded with a
happy company—of friends, and dear ones
loved and lost; they crowd around my way
—and beckon me to follow down the
paths of yesterday.

The present seems to vanish, for the past is
real again: the sunny times, the stormy
times, the pleasure and the pain—but soon
my mind is haunted by lost dreams and vain
regret remembering the things that I have
wanted to forget.

Close the Gates of Memory. Come back, my
heart, come back. You dare not go too far
along that old forgotten track . . . Keep
sacred every well-loved name but cling
not to the sorrow—lest you miss the way
that leads you forward to Tomorrow.

Trees Take Time

Trees take time to grow. They can't be
hurried. Slow but sure—they gain in
strength and height and girth and patiently
endure—the fury of the winter storms, and
as the years pass by—roots go deeper,
boughs grow wider, reaching for the sky.

Souls, like trees, take time to grow. The
pace you cannot force. Every problem must
be faced and life must take its course . . .
Day by day you have to learn to stand up
strong and straight—arms outspread to
greet the sun whatever be your fate.

Do not give up in despair when courage
seems to fail. Learn to hold on by the roots
unshaken by the gale. When you see a
lovely tree—a giant it may appear—But
don't forget it only grew a little year by
year.

Everything Comes Back

One way or another everything comes
back: the pain you cause for others, the
unprovoked attack—the little hurts
inflicted by what you do or say—come back
in full measure, somehow, somewhere,
someday.

The unkind word repeated, the cruel
sentence said—unfairness and ingratitude
come back upon your head—for that's the
way things happen for you and everyone.
Soon or late we suffer for harm that we
have done.

But good as well as evil its own reward will
bring. The gift, the selfless action, the
charitable thing—return to you as surely as
comets in their track. One way or another—
everything comes back.